Fun with
Shapes

 Belitha Press

First published in the UK in 1998 by

Belitha Press Limited,
London House, Great Eastern Wharf
Parkgate Road, London SW11 4NQ

ISBN 1 85561 769 2

British Library Cataloguing in Publication Data for
this book is available from the British Library.

Printed in Hong Kong

Series editor: Honor Head
Series designer: Jamie Asher
Illustrator: Brigitte McDonald

Shapes

written by
Peter Patilla

illustrated by
Brigitte McDonald

About this book

Fun with Shapes will help children to explore the exciting world of shapes. The wide variety of exercises will show children that there are many different types of shape. The puzzles introduce natural shapes such as the moon and stars, manufactured shapes, such as boxes, and geometric shapes, such as circles, cubes and rectangles. The games and puzzles will also help children to recognize and name a range of shapes and to be aware of the shapes around them in their everyday lives.

Confident children will enjoy tackling the puzzles at their own pace. You can help less confident children by going through the book with them and talking about each puzzle before they begin to solve it. If the children give a wrong answer, explain why it is wrong and encourage them to start again.

Contents

Mystery Gifts

Can you name the presents which have been wrapped up?

Can you find the teddy bear?
Can you find the aeroplane?
Can you find the bucket?

Viewpoints

Name these objects. Can you find them in the big picture?

Spot the Difference

Look at the house in these pictures.

Can you spot 8 differences?

Top to Bottom

Look at the shapes, sizes and patterns of these boxes. Can you match the tops to the bottoms?

Feast of Fun

Find the odd shape out in each group. Why is it odd?

Sky Gazing

How many of these shapes can you find in the picture?

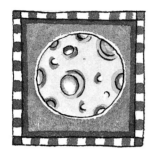   

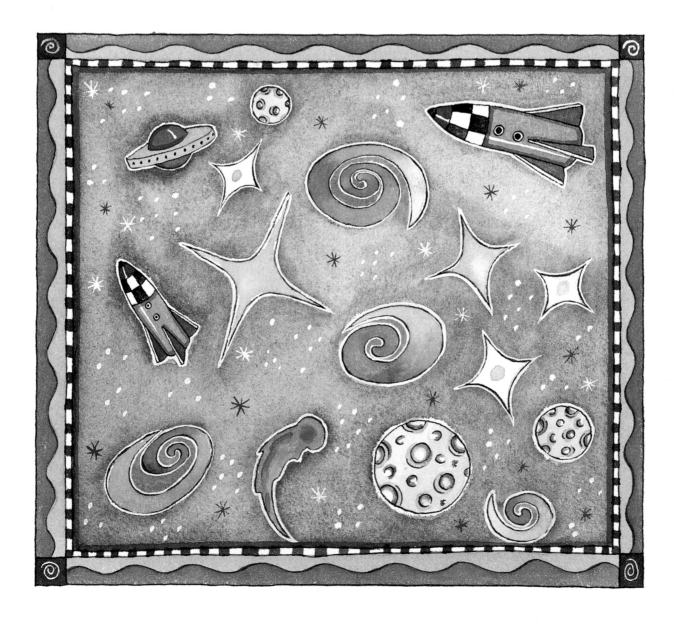

How many of these shapes can you find?

Set and Match

Find a set of three cards with the same shape on the opposite page and match it with a shape below.

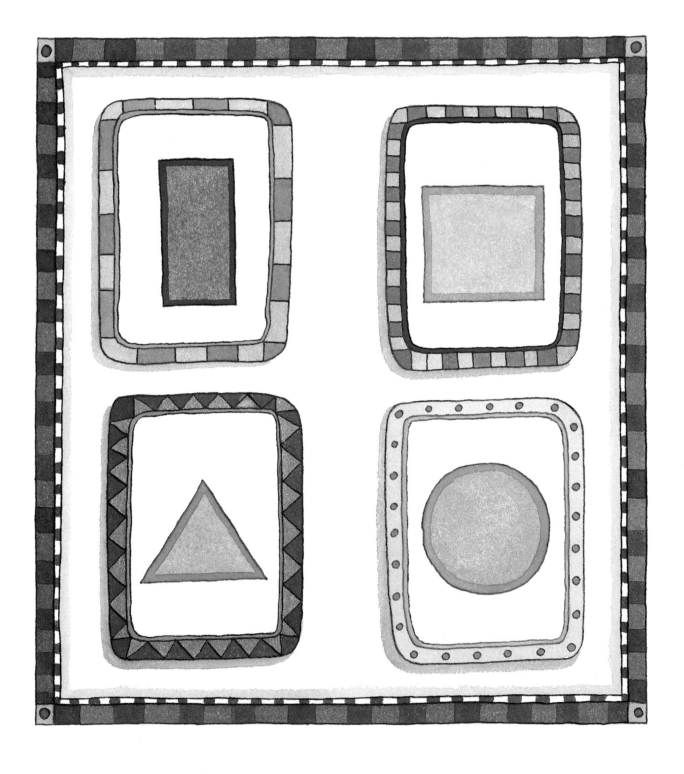

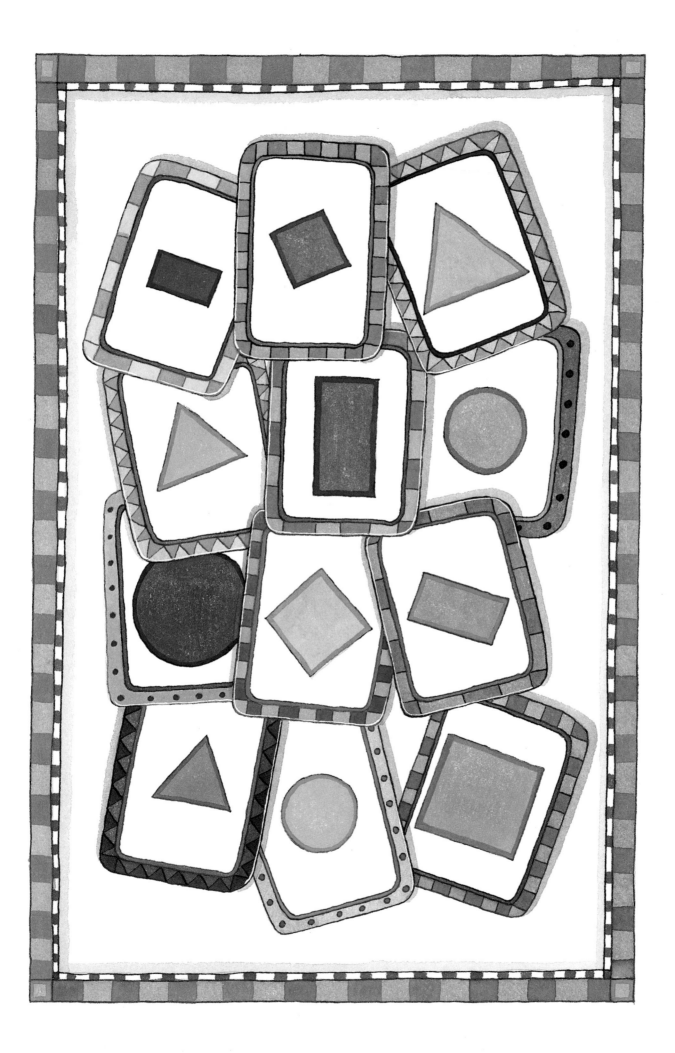

Shape Spotting

How many of these shapes can you find in the pictures?

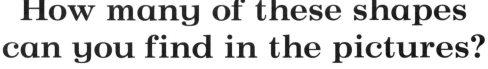

Amazing Shapes

Match the shapes at each end of the paths by following the same shapes through the maze.

Match the Shapes

Where does each shape fit?

Pipework

How many of these shapes can you see in the pipes below?

squares

rectangles

circles

triangles

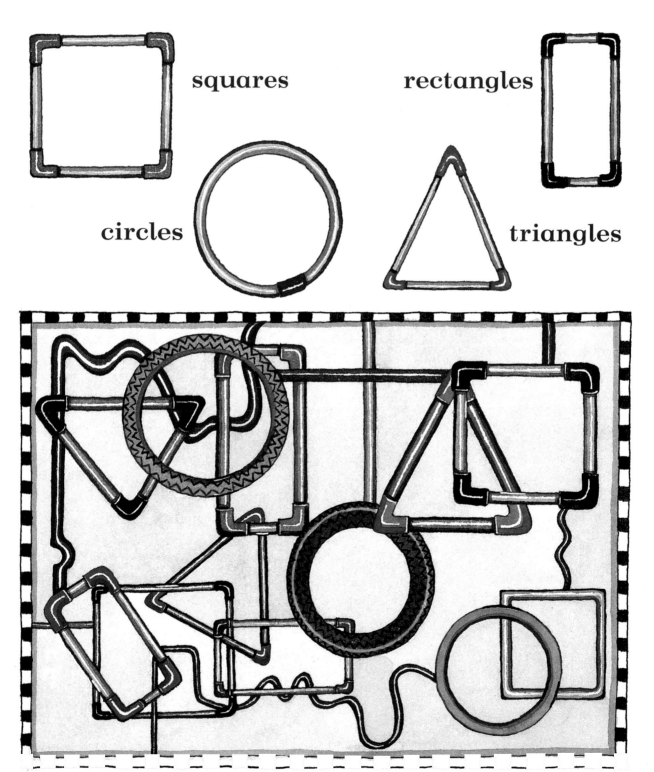

Shape Snap

Choose a shape below. Find a matching card and say 'snap!'

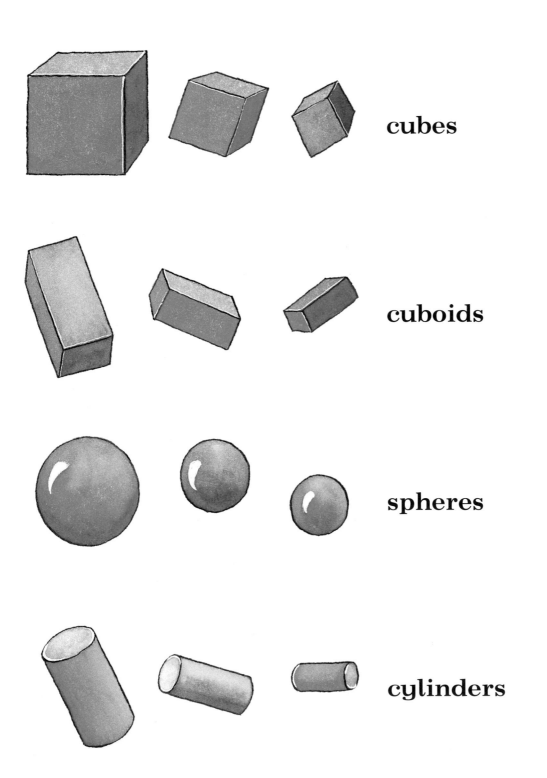

cubes

cuboids

spheres

cylinders

Up and Away

Can you find the shapes below in the picture?

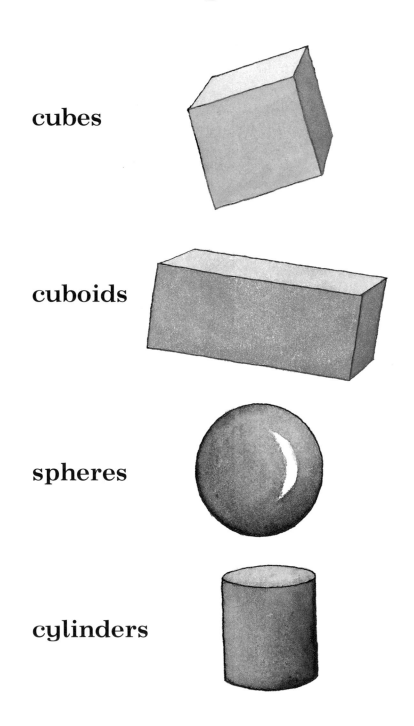

cubes

cuboids

spheres

cylinders

Lorry Loads

Can you find the odd shape out in each lorry load? What is the name of the odd shape?

Shapes

square

circle

triangle

rectangle

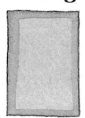

cube

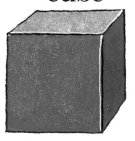

sphere

cylinder

cuboid